D0685122

THE LITTLE BOOK OF TWITTER

TIM COLLINS

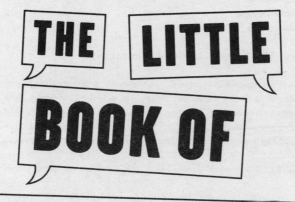

THE LITTLE

BOOK OF

TWITTER

MICHAEL O'MARA BOOKS LIMITED

First published in Great Britain in 2009 by
Michael O'Mara Books Limited
9 Lion Yard
Tremadoc Road
London SW4 7NQ

A CIP catalogue record for this book is available from the British Library.

Papers used by Michael O'Mara Books Limited are natural, recyclable products
made from wood grown in sustainable forests. The manufacturing processes
conform to the environmental regulations of the country of origin.

ISBN: 978-1-84317-405-9

1 2 3 4 5 6 7 8 9 10

www.mombooks.com

Cover design by Allan Sommerville

Design and typesetting by Sailesh Patel

Printed and bound in Great Britain by Cox and Wyman, Reading, Berks.

Contents

Acknowledgements

Thanks to Collette Collins, Emily Dent, Kathryn Partridge, Lindsay Davies, Kerry Chapple, Ana Sampson and Louise Dixon. Thanks also to @ljrich for her helpful Twitter know-how.

For more info, tweet @OMaraBooks or @TheLittleBookOf

8

Foretweet

Twitter is a social networking site with a 140-character limit, which means that you don't have to put up with long-winded sentences like th

Introduction

On Tuesday the 3rd of February 2009, Stephen Fry got stuck in a lift. At first, this might not have seemed like a generation-defining event on a par with the Kennedy assassination and the moon landing. But this is how future generations will probably remember it, because this was the moment when Twitter went mainstream. Tweeting to his followers on his phone, Fry turned a mundane inconvenience into a gripping drama with updates such as 'Hell's teeth' and 'Arse, poo and widdle'. The next day, Fry's updates, and the responses of his hundreds of thousands of followers, were reported in newspapers and on websites around the world.

It was at this moment that Twitter became the social networking platform we were all supposed to know about. Suddenly, Facebook and MySpace seemed about as fashionable as bright green shellsuits, and admitting that you didn't know what a tweet was was like admitting you didn't know where babies came from.

10

In a state of panic, we all signed up to Twitter, worried that the zeitgeist train would leave without us and we'd be left with less technological relevancy than an old man buying cassettes from a charity shop.

The first reaction of many upon seeing the site was relief. There were no zombie applications, no gifts, no terrible music and no embedded junk to crash our browsers. Instead, there were 'tweets'; mini-updates of no more than 140 characters. Twitter was a site that understood a fundamental truth about our modern online requirements – less is more. We live in times of cultural overload, where we're all required to be familiar with so many albums, books, movies, blogs, DVD box sets, games, Blu Rays and iPhone apps that it's a wonder we have time to sleep. The last thing we need is another essential cultural phenomenon that will eat even further into our waking moments. But updates of about twenty words? Yeah, we can probably fit that in.

Going on Facebook is like attending a school reunion where all the people you used to sit next to in maths poke you and wave embarrassing photos in your face. Going on MySpace is like visiting a hall of residence where every single room is inhabited by douchebags who think that writing tortured acoustic songs will impress the girls. But Twitter is more like a dinner party that you can invite anyone to, from your best friend to the editor of your favourite magazine to Snoop Dogg. It's pretty much the only social networking site you'd want to visit in real life.

So, welcome to the twitterverse. Whether you're a twittern00b or a twitterholic, I hope you'll find this guide to be a fitting celebration of what is undoubtedly the greatest social networking service in the world. (Until they invent one that restricts updates to ten characters and we all flock to that one instead.)

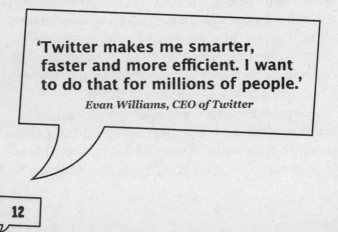

'Twitter makes me smarter, faster and more efficient. I want to do that for millions of people.'

Evan Williams, CEO of Twitter

Everything you need to know about Twitter in ten tweets

Welcome to *The Little Book of Twitter*, a short guide to getting the most out of the micro-blogging phenomenon Twitter. If this fast-paced digital age has depleted your attention span so much that even a book of this size seems too long, here are the fundamentals of Twitter boiled down to ten tweets.

1

thelittlebookoftwitter **Twitter**
is a social networking site that
lets you record your thoughts
in 'tweets', small updates of
140 characters or fewer.

about one minute ago

2

thelittlebookoftwitter **Go to Twitter.com to register. You can upload a profile picture, post a mini biography and change the background design of your homepage.**

about two minutes ago

3

thelittlebookoftwitter **You can use Twitter to communicate with people you know, find new people who interest you, or both.**

about three minutes ago

4

thelittlebookoftwitter Use the 'Find People' option to search for profiles, and then click on 'Follow'.

about four minutes ago

5

thelittlebookoftwitter **To reply to a tweet, type '@' followed by the person's username, or click on the arrow that appears on the right when you roll over it.**

about five minutes ago

6

thelittlebookoftwitter **If someone posts an update or link you want to share, type 'RT' (retweet) followed by '@' and their username, then copy and paste it.**

about six minutes ago

7

thelittlebookoftwitter **Desktop
applications such as TweetDeck
(which you can download from
tweetdeck.com) will help you
get more out of Twitter.**

about seven minutes ago

8

thelittlebookoftwitter Tweeting gets even more addictive when you do it from your phone. You can tweet by SMS or via your phone's 3G or Wi-Fi connection.

about eight minutes ago

9

thelittlebookoftwitter There are all sorts of fun tools that can make Twitter more interesting, such as Twitpic, which lets you share photos in your tweets.

about nine minutes ago

10

thelittlebookoftwitter **Keep your tweets interesting, send lots of @ replies, and soon you'll be a bigger Internet celebrity than the sneezing panda.**

about ten minutes ago

How to tweet

Twitter is a service that lets you send small updates to your friends, your family, your colleagues and, if you like, complete strangers. All of these updates are, in theory, responses to the question 'What are you doing?', using 140 characters or fewer. The concept is brilliantly simple, and so is the process. Go to Twitter.com, sign up and you can be tweeting in seconds. If getting started on Twitter needed much more explanation than that, it's unlikely that it would have had its phenomenal success. However, there are a few things you should know when setting out.

Signing up

To join, go to Twitter.com and click on 'Get started'. You will be asked to enter your name, username and password. Unless you're the offspring of a rock star and have a name like Pixie Apple Moonbase, it's likely that your real name will have been taken, and you'll have to think up a username. It's

24

probably better not to go too comedy with this. 'Slutbitchwhore' might be an amusing username for a couple of weeks, but the joke will start to wear thin when your mum starts following you. Unless her username is 'Whorebitchslut', of course.

Twitter will then ask if it can search through your email address book to find your friends, and let you search the site for people to follow. It will also give you an option to link Twitter to your mobile phone for SMS updates. After that, you can compose your first tweet, which might well be something along the lines of, 'Just experimenting with this new-fangled Twitter thingummybob.' There's no right or wrong way to tweet, but don't assume that all your tweets have to be earth-shatteringly witty or intelligent. If that were the case, Ashton Kutcher wouldn't have millions of followers.

Once you've decided what to tweet, type it in the textbox underneath the question, 'What are you doing?' As you type, you'll notice the counter above the textbox going down, to tell you how many characters you've got left before you reach the limit. If this goes into minus figures, you've written too much and you won't be able to post your update. Take a quick look back over your words and ~~try your best to~~ see if you can ~~possibly afford to~~ ditch any of them ~~without changing the meaning of what you've written~~.

Advanced tweeting

On your homepage, you'll see the most recent tweets of people you're following. Roll over them and you'll see a couple of symbols. The first is a star, and clicking on it will add the tweet to your 'Favourites' folder, which is useful if it contains a link you want to look at later. Underneath this is an arrow, which lets you reply to the tweet. If you click on it, '@' followed by the username of the twitterer will appear in your textbox, and you should type your reply after it. You can also type '@' followed by someone's username if you want them to know you're mentioning them in a tweet. You can send private messages to people who are following you by clicking on 'Message' in their profile.

Including links in your tweets is straightforward. Just type or paste a web address in, and Twitter will automatically turn it into a hyperlink. And because you don't want web addresses eating into your precious character limit, Twitter uses the TinyURL service to shorten the link. Copy and paste a long link and it will appear in your tweet as a tinyurl.com address.

Privacy settings

Just tweeted about how you're going to pull a sickie because it's Friday and the weather's nice, and then remembered that your boss is following you? No problem. You can roll over any of the tweets on your profile page and click on the trash icon to delete them.

If you think you'll be prone to these kind of 'mistweets', or you're not comfortable with sharing all your updates publicly, you can make your account private by clicking on 'Settings' and then checking the 'Protect my updates' box at the bottom of the page. That way only approved followers will be able to see your tweets, so as long as you don't say anything unpleasant about them, you should be able to stay out of trouble.

Understanding your homepage

The tweets you see in the timeline on your homepage might seem a little obscure at first, especially those with the '@' symbol in, which could be replies to updates you haven't read in the first place. You'll also see the abbreviation 'RT' a lot. This stands for 'retweet', and is like the Twitter equivalent of forwarding an email. If you see a tweet that you think will be worth sharing with your followers, such as an especially witty comment or a useful link, retweet it by typing 'RT' then '@' followed by the username of the person you're quoting before repeating their tweet.

Another symbol you'll see a lot of is '#', which will appear before a word or phrase, as in '#followfriday'. These are known as hashtags, and tweeters use them to make it easier to search for the topic they're writing about. If you type a hashtag in your tweet, it will create a link that takes people to all the other recent tweets on the same subject.

If sending @ replies, retweeting and shrinking URLs sounds like too much effort, you can download a desktop client like Tweetdeck (see the 'Twitter tools' chapter) that will make these things easier.

Customizing your profile

Before you get too immersed in tweeting, you might want to take a moment to customize your profile. To do this, you'll have to click on 'Settings' underneath your username on your homepage. Mercifully, users aren't given too many options to customize their profile. If the web has taught us anything, it's that people will make things unpleasantly messy if they're given the option. If they can use an eye-bogglingly naff typeface like Comic Sans, they will. If they can embed videos of otters holding hands, they will. And if they can make death metal automatically play at ear-melting volume, they will. So your customization options on Twitter are limited to things such as a photo, the URL of your website or blog, background design and a bio of 160 characters or fewer.

Photos and bios

It's probably best to play it straight when it comes to these options. Photos on Twitter appear pretty small, especially for mobile users, so posting a simple portrait shot will help people work out if they know you or not. You might think that posting a picture of yourself in an exotic environment or with a celebrity might make you more interesting to potential followers but these images will be pretty obscure when reduced to a size smaller than a square centimetre. You should also avoid posting a picture of a semi-naked woman and then adding a link to the breakthrough product you're selling in every tweet, as you'll get blocked for spamming. I know this is unfair on genuine semi-naked women who've invented breakthrough products, but those are the rules.

Posting a straight and factual description of yourself in your bio is also a good idea. Anyone who types words such as 'astronaut', 'contract killer' or 'gigolo' in this section should automatically have them translated as 'office joker'. As for background design, you can choose from one of Twitter's tasteful options or upload your own image. If you're choosing the latter option, try and resist the 'tile' option unless you want your homepage to descend into MySpace garishness. Alternatively, you could go to sites such as twitterbacks.com, tweetstyle.com and twitbacks.com and create your own customized backgrounds. But, please, for the sake of our poor eyes, don't pimp them up too much.

And that's pretty much all you need to know to get started. So don't just sit there – tweet something.

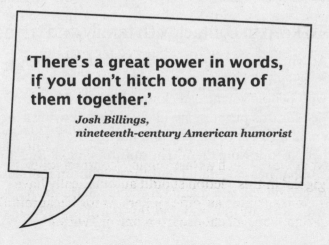

'There's a great power in words, if you don't hitch too many of them together.'

Josh Billings,
nineteenth-century American humorist

How do you want to use Twitter?

Some people might tell you that there's a right or wrong way to use Twitter, but the truth is that it can be used in several different ways. Here are a few reasons you might have for entering the twittersphere.

To keep in contact with family and friends

As with other social networking platforms such as Facebook, Twitter can be used to stay in contact with people you already know. People who use it just for this purpose are likely to be following a small number of people, and have a small number of people following them. The anthropologist Richard Dunbar has calculated that the maximum number of people you can maintain stable relationships with is about 150, and that this is a 'direct function of relative neocortex size'. So next time you want to block someone you don't like, blame it on your neocortex.

To meet new people

Alternatively, you could be using Twitter to make friends with people around the world who have similar interests, to meet new business contacts, or even as a dating site. Although this latter option might not work if you're a beautiful Asian woman, as people will assume you're a fake account invented to spam.

As a promotional tool

Many people use Twitter to promote a blog, a website or a product. They range from people who have something genuinely useful to offer, to people who message you every three seconds with a link to their revolutionary new method for earning six figures in twelve hours.

To follow the updates of others

Since the celebrity invasion of Twitter, some users have signed up just to follow notable people. The technical term for these people is 'lurkers' rather than 'stalkers', although neither sounds very nice. Techie types will tell lurkers that they're betraying the principle of interactivity in social networking, but lurkers will be too busy following P Diddy's tantric sex updates to care.

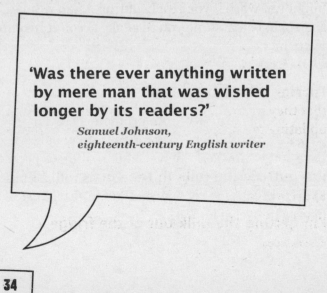

'Was there ever anything written by mere man that was wished longer by its readers?'

Samuel Johnson,
eighteenth-century English writer

The netiquette of Twitter

Given the diverse groups of people using Twitter, it's no surprise that there's little consensus about the exact rules of it. But there are a few general principles that you should be aware of if you want to avoid annoying everyone and getting 'unfollowed'.

Don't overtweet

Looking at some people's profiles, it's a wonder that they manage to type anything other than 'I'm updating my status on Twitter'. We've all had tweets like this clogging our timelines:

I'm putting the milk in the coffee.

4 seconds ago

I'm getting the milk out of the fridge.

5 seconds ago

I'm putting sugar in the coffee.

6 seconds ago

I'm pouring a cup of coffee.

7 seconds ago

How do these people do it? Have they trained themselves to perform everyday tasks with their feet, like people who've suffered industrial accidents?

While the ordinary details of your daily existence can be just as interesting as the more important things in your life, an unrelenting stream of mundane tweets will lead to mass unfollowing.

Only you can judge how many tweets your followers want to hear, but generally speaking, more than one tweet an hour might be considered overtweeting. Unless you're Jack Bauer, and lots of exciting things happen to you every hour.

Don't undertweet

On the other hand, it's unlikely that you'll make much of an impression if you only tweet once a week or so. You might not want to use Twitter for anything more than following Snoop Dogg's updizzles, but you won't get the full experience, and understand what all the fuss is about, until you join in.

Don't worry about answering the question 'What are you doing?'

Twitter purists will tell you that tweets should only ever take the form of a response to the question written above the textbox. But this isn't how most people use the site now, and it's better for it. Tweets can be jokes, observations, links, haikus, comments on news events or questions. Whatever you think people will want to read.

Don't go overboard with abbreviations

While it's always tempting to stuff abbreviations
and acronyms into tweets, including too many goes
against the principles of micro-blogging, which
forces you to say what you mean in as few words as
possible. So IMHO, going OTT with acronyms will
make you a PITA.

Don't boast

Much as we'll all be pleased to hear your good
news, try not to let your tweets descend into
a string of self-aggrandizing boasts, unless
you're a gangsta rapper and your fans would be
disappointed with anything less. Make it more
interesting for your followers by tweeting about
your frustrations as well as your successes. Or
least disguise your bragging as self-deprecation. So
rather than tweeting, 'I'm throwing a dinner party
for Bono, Angelina Jolie and Barack Obama', try
'I'm throwing a dinner party for Bono, Angelina
Jolie and Barack Obama and I've just totally burnt
the fishcakes – what an idiot I am!'

Don't tweet about how many followers you have

A very specific type of boasting that should be avoided on Twitter is enthusiastically tweeting about how many followers you've got. These kind of tweets tend to be self-congratulatory announcements about milestones you've passed, like attaining 1000 followers. Do this and you'll only make yourself look like an excitable child who's playing a numbers game and isn't really interested in what anyone has to say. You might even find that number of followers you're so proud of mysteriously depleting.

Don't post updates that span more than one tweet

The very reason why Twitter has become so popular is that it forces brevity. If you can't cope with this, stay away. Few things break the netiquette of Twitter more than continuing your post over multiple tweets. If your post is too long-winded for Twitter, stick it on your blog and we'll ignore it there. By splitting sentences into multiple tweets you'll annoy Twitter purists, and you might even change the meaning of your messages by mistake. For example, imagine you want to send this message:

@username I really hope you get a chance to come up and visit us this year!!! It's been a while since you were here and your mother is dying to see you!!!

If you're in the habit of cutting sentences off at the character limit, the first tweet the person will see is:

@username I really hope you get a chance to come up and visit us this year!!! It's been a while since you were here and your mother is dying

Chop out extraneous words, keep it all in one tweet, and avoid distressing situations like this.

Don't try to use up the whole 140 characters every single time

Some people seem to think that 140 characters is both the maximum and the minimum on Twitter, and fill up their tweets with exclamation marks and LOLs until they've reached the limit. If you're going to pad things out, at least be deliberately annoying and add the words 'and tweeting about it' to every single update.

Be subtle with your plugs

Twitter is a great tool for promoting your blog, your website or even your product, unless your product is a fake Rolex or new penis-enlargement technology, but you should show some restraint when plugging. If you tweet over and over again about how we should vote for your blog on Digg, you'll be unfollowed quicker than a Nigerian millionaire asking for bank account details.

Give a bit of explanation for your links

Most people will see a lot of links in their timelines, so you need to give some explanation as to why they should make the effort to click on the one you're posting. If you type, 'This is so cool!!! http://tinyurl.com/etc', your link might pass by unclicked. For all we know, you might be the kind of person who thinks that the sex tape of 'Screech' from *Saved by the Bell* is cool.

Don't @ message someone to tell them you've just sent them a direct message

You might be keen to draw someone's attention to the message you've just sent, but doing so in an @ message will simply make everyone else curious about what the private message was. This is the online equivalent of writing a note for your best friend in school and not letting anyone else read it.

Retweet instead of passing off the tweets of others as your own

If someone you're following has tweeted something especially hilarious, insightful or accurate, don't tweet exactly the same thing yourself. If you think an update or link deserves a wider audience, retweet it by typing 'RT' followed by '@' and the person's username before repeating their words.

Don't retweet everything in your feed

On the other hand, don't go overboard with retweeting. It's unlikely that everything in your timeline deserves a wider audience. Plus, if everything you ever send begins with 'RT', you might look like you've got no thoughts of your own.

Don't send everyone who follows you an automatic message of thanks

If you know someone in real life and they start following you, there's no reason you shouldn't

43

send them a quick message of thanks. But don't feel like you have to join in the trend of sending an automatic thank-you message to anyone who starts following you. These can get annoying, especially for people who get their direct messages sent by SMS, and have just gone to all the effort of taking their phone out of their pocket to read your generic thanks. It's probably better to buck the trend by sending an automatic rude message to new followers like, 'Excuse me, do I know you?'

Don't drink and tweet

Stay away from Twitter in that dangerous window when you're drunk enough to think everything in your head is hilarious and fascinating, but you're not too drunk to type. It's like drunk-dialling thousands of people at once. Oh, and if you're a rock star who's using Twitter to communicate with your fan base, remember this advice applies when using hard drugs too.

Don't tweet about going to the toilet

I know your time on the throne might be the only chance you get to look at Twitter on your phone, but can't you just pretend that you're somewhere else? Some of us are trying to eat.

Don't tweet if nothing whatsoever has changed in your life since your last tweet

If you're going to use tweets as status updates, you should probably wait until your status actually changes before posting them. This is a social networking site, not a challenging Samuel Beckett monologue . . .

Still pretty much right here on my office chair.

about ten minutes ago

Still sitting at my desk in the office.

about two hours ago

Sitting at my desk in the office.

about four hours ago

I understand that you have more time to tweet when you're clock-watching at work than when you're out partying hard, but at least try and post an interesting link or something.

Don't only send @ replies to celebrities

There's nothing wrong with following celebrities on Twitter, despite what techie purists might tell you. And if you send an @ reply to a celebrity's tweet, they might reply back and make your day. But if these are your only interactions on Twitter, it can look a little sad. You might think that you look like a badass playa if you only ever tweet things like '@britneyspears Great show tonight Brit', '@stephenfry LOL!!!' or '@snoopdogg FO SHIZZLE MY NIZZLE!' But to everyone else you'll look like a sad fan hanging around outside the stage door on your own.

Restrict boring conversations to direct messages

If you're arranging when and where to meet your girlfriend tonight, stick it in a direct message rather than an @ message. These replies will clog up the timelines of your followers who won't be especially interested in overhearing your conversation.
On the other hand, if you want to have a blazing row accusing her of infidelity, use @ messages by all means. We don't mind overhearing private conversations if they're of the Jerry Springer variety.

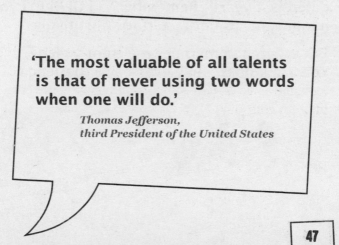

'The most valuable of all talents is that of never using two words when one will do.'

Thomas Jefferson,
third President of the United States

Don't put personal things in @ messages

Remember that @ messages are public and will show up in the profile of the person you're sending them to. If you think the content of your message might be sensitive, put it in a direct message instead. For example, the following kinds of tweet should probably be kept private:

@username There's no reason for her to find out about last night. Just say you were staying with a friend.

@username Hey, it's me!!! How R U??? We dated last year!!! Remember??? LOL!!! FYI you might want to get tested for Chlamydia.

@username Remember me from college? You are still my only ever gay experience.

Be careful about broadcasting details of social gatherings

Social networking sites have been responsible for a lot of unintentional shit stirring, and Twitter is no exception. For example, if you're planning to attend someone's party, think twice before you tweet about it. Will your post be seen by someone who'll be offended that they weren't invited? Do you have a bunch of nerdy friends who are likely to turn up uninvited and kill the buzz with their sheer dorkiness? To be on the safe side, you should restrict your communication on the subject to direct messages.

Avoid passé Internet memes

An Internet meme is a catchphrase, site or viral clip that spreads quickly from person to person via email, blog, message board or social networking site. They are essentially in-jokes, and like all in-jokes they run their course after a while, so make sure you're not still spreading them when the moment has well and truly passed. We've all seen the sneezing panda clip by now,

49

and if you write, 'This is so cool! LOL!' and link to it, it could dent your online credibility. The same goes for LOLcats, Star Wars Kid, Peanut Butter Jelly Time, Dramatic Chipmunk and Diet Coke and Mentos, great contributions to our culture though they are.

Don't tweet when someone is talking to you in real life

I know that you're perfectly capable of multitasking, but there are some people who still get upset if you look at your phone or computer screen when they're speaking to you. Luddites.

Don't tweet at someone who's sitting next to you

When you're about to send a tweet to someone, it's always worth looking up from your phone or computer. Are they sitting right next to you? Perhaps it would be better to talk to them. Oh, and you just might be getting dangerously addicted.

Ten reasons why Twitter is the best social networking site

Boiling social networking down to short messages has given Twitter a simplicity that won't be beaten until they plant chips in all our heads that let us transmit updates telepathically. Here are ten reasons why Twitter is better than other social networking services.

1. It forces brevity

Twitter's 140-character limit is a stroke of genius because it acknowledges that in our age of information overload we only read the first sentence of most things anyway. By which token you've all given up on this section by now and I might as well make the rest of it about the history of livestock-breeding in Uzbekistan.

The only downside to the limit is that it can't be enforced in real life. Satisfying though it would be to cut off a dull meeting contribution or windy anecdote mid-flow, telling someone that they've reached their character limit isn't socially acceptable just yet.

2. You don't feel obliged to respond to everyone all the time

Twitter is the social networking service that you can tune in and out of as the mood takes you. The others start off as enjoyable novelties but soon descend into just another inbox of stuff you've got to get round to ploughing through. The first time a work acquaintance challenged you to a game of Facebook Scrabble it might have been exciting, but a couple of games later you're clicking 'Accept' just because you don't want to offend them. And then there are those 258 'Other requests' you haven't even looked at yet…

3. You won't get bitten by a vampire or a zombie

Oh, how we laughed when we were first invited to add Facebook's vampire application! And then the zombie one. And then the aquarium one. And then the Lego one. And then the fortune cookie one. And then the Pokemon one. And then the food fight one. And then the Pac-Man one. And then the Chuck Norris one. Eventually, going on Facebook became like being cornered by David Brent or Michael Scott at the Christmas party.

4. You won't get asked to join pointless groups

The 'Groups' function on Facebook was a good idea for meeting people with the same interests, but it was destined to fall into the hands of idiots. Now every time you check Facebook you see twenty new time-wasting invites:

GROUP: If 1,000,000 people join this group I'll run naked down the High Street!!!
SIZE: 127 members   TYPE: Just for fun

GROUP: I hate the new Facebook!!!
SIZE: 47 members   TYPE: Just for fun

GROUP: Let's make this the biggest group on Facebook!!!
SIZE: 236 members   TYPE: Just for fun

I've got an idea. How about an application that blocks anyone who's ever clicked the 'just for fun' option and prevents them from ever being able to contact you in any way ever again?

5. Your friends won't show everyone you know a photograph of you covered in sick

Well, they could do, I suppose. They could tweet something like, 'LOL look at @username being sick down his trousers http//twitpic.com/etc.' But this would make them look like they were really going out of their way to be unpleasant. On Facebook, however, no one would think twice about uploading all their snaps from last night's party, tagging you in them, and making that photograph of you asleep on the toilet floor with your hand still grasping a bottle of vodka appear on the homepage of everyone you've ever met.

6. You don't have to describe your relationship with someone you want to follow

Your only social interaction with Gary from Finance was a brief and awkward conversation at the office away day. However, he's decided it would be funny if he describes your relationship on Facebook as 'We met randomly, we hooked up, we travelled together, we are in the same family and I don't even know this person'. And you've got to confirm this japery or risk upsetting him.

7. It doesn't keep showing you pictures of people you may know

The 'People you may know' feature on Facebook seems to have been designed especially to create social networking awkwardness. It generates a list of people you have a lot of mutual friends with and shows pictures of them on the top right corner of your homepage. Just to keep Facebook quiet, you make friends with the ones you vaguely know, leaving just people you either don't know or don't like. These social leftovers will then be rotated on your homepage so regularly that you see them more often than your friends. Come on Facebook, take the hint. We're not interested.

8. You won't be subjected to a sub-James Blunt acoustic track when you look at someone's profile

Advocates of MySpace will tend to tell you that it's the social networking option of choice for creative people. Which sounds great in theory, but is often unpleasant in practice. You meet someone who seems nice enough. But when you check out their MySpace page like you said you would, it turns out that they're capable of creating noises with just their voice and a guitar that could be used as instruments of torture. And the worst thing is, this atrocious noise appears as soon as you look at the page, without you ever having asked to listen to it.

9. You can't embed an animated picture of a kitten holding a glittery love heart on your profile page

Even if you manage to turn the music down on MySpace you won't be able to protect your eyes from all the crap that's embedded there. Most profile pages are so overloaded with animated GIFs, blinkies, moving avatars, emoticons, glitter graphics and YouTube videos that looking at them for more than three seconds means you have to take a couple of headache pills and lie down. Being on MySpace might be acceptable if you're a hyperactive child on Lucozade who thinks that clipart of rainbows is cute, but being on there when you're an adult is just creepy.

10. You can pretend that you're friends with celebrities

Okay, okay. I realize that this does sort of make Twitter sound like a stalker's site, which is exactly what its detractors claim. But it's a pretty mild form of stalking if this is true. There's a significant line between reading that a celebrity has just arrived back at their Beverly Hills mansion and popping up there to rifle through their bins, and I'm happy to say it's one I've yet to cross.

Anyway, it's interesting to see tweets from your friends mixing in with tweets from celebrities. It helps you realize that we all experience a similar day-to-day reality. They just experience it while reclining in Jacuzzis full of Cristal aboard private yachts.

Tweologisms

By law, every article written about Twitter has to feature a few invented words beginning with the letters 't' and 'w', or 'tweologisms' as I like to call them. Here are a few examples of these buzzwords.

The twitterati – either used to describe celebrities who tweet, or others who've amassed so many followers they've become Twitter celebrities.

The tweet elite – people who attract hundreds of thousands of followers.

Tweeps/tweeple/twittizens/tweeters – people who use Twitter. NB Rarely 'twits'.

Twitticism – a bon mot of less than 140 characters.

Twittervangelist – someone who wants to convert everyone they meet to Twitter.

Twitterholic – someone with a tweeting problem.

Twitthore – someone who follows others indiscriminately.

Twaddict – a twitter addict. Hooked, but not a full-blown twitterholic yet.

Twitter diet – when a twitterholic tries to cut down on their tweets.

Twitterquette/twetiquette – the etiquette of using Twitter.

Twitterstalker – someone who finds your tweets a bit too interesting.

Twitterjacking – pretending to be someone else, usually a celebrity, by updating a fake account.

Twittersquatting – registering a Twitter ID like Nike, Pepsi or Coke in the hope that you might be able to sell it one day.

Tweetup – a real-life meeting between two or more people who've got to know each other on Twitter. You might have to temporarily suspend the 140 character limit for these, unless you're especially good at counting.

Twitteristics – your activity profile on Twitter: how often you tweet, how often you reply, and how likely you are to follow someone one back.

Twitterstream – the list of updates of those you follow that appears on your homepage.

Twired – so over-stimulated from tweeting that you can't sleep.

Tweetwise – versed in the etiquette of Twitter.

Tweetworthy – something you deem to be worthy of an update. Some believe that only life-changing events are tweetworthy. Others believe that choosing between tall, grande and venti is good for at least five updates.

Twittersona – a persona you've created for Twitter. The people who update the accounts of Jesus, God and Satan have presumably created Twittersonas.

Twittern00b – a newbie on Twitter. Derived from the web slang 'n00b', for a clueless newcomer. If you didn't know what a n00b was, you probably are one.

61

Other jargon

Not all of the jargon you'll need to know when using Twitter begins with 'Tw' just yet. Here are a few other terms that you might encounter.

The fail whale - the illustration of a whale being lifted out of the sea by birds that Twitter displays when its servers are overloaded. This picture means that you'll have to stop tweeting for an hour or two. To twitterholics, this sight is as disturbing and upsetting as Freddy Krueger appearing in their bedroom at night.

Unfollow - remove someone's updates from your timeline by clicking on this option on their profile. This rejection is feared by twitterholics, who will wonder what they're doing wrong.

Noise ratio - your ratio of followers to updates. Someone who updates often but has few followers would be said to have a noisy account. Not to be confused with a noisy MySpace account, which is one that automatically plays Slipknot at full blast.

Hashtag - a word or phrase preceded by the '#' symbol. Tweeters include these to make it easier for those reading their updates to search for particular subjects. You can keep track of the most popular hashtags at www.hashtags. org. Note that if you're using a Mac with a UK keyboard, you'll have to press 'Alt' and '3' to type the hash symbol.

Nudge - a note that you can request Twitter to send to someone's phone to remind them that they haven't tweeted for a while. If you think someone's left it too long since their last update, click on the 'Nudge' button on their profile, and they'll get a message saying, 'You've been nudged! [username] wants to know what you're doing.' Try to resist this if your friend's deliberately avoiding Twitter because they're addicted, though. That would be like leaving a surprise tequila shot on an alcoholic's desk.

Follow Friday – the tradition of suggesting new people to follow on a Friday. To participate, tweet the hashtag '#followfriday' and then the usernames you want to recommend. Similar traditions that users have tried to instigate include '#musicmonday', '#tweetuptuesday', '#myfavouritethingsthursday' and '#woofwednesday', for dogs with their own Twitter accounts.

Ghost-tweeters – PR people who update the accounts of celebrities on their behalf.

Broadcaster – someone who uses Twitter mainly to post updates rather than to engage with others.

Responder – someone who uses Twitter mainly to reply to others rather than post updates.

Lurker – someone who uses Twitter mainly to read the tweets of others rather than to post their own updates.

Spammer – someone using Twitter to aggressively plug anything from a website to some dodgy herbal medicine.

Troll – someone who posts controversial or inflammatory messages in an online community just to get a reaction. These people are the reason why Twitter gives you the option to block users on their profile pages.

Dweet – a tweet sent while drunk.

Lifestreaming – tweeting every single detail of what you do in your life. Critics of Twitter claim that the site is only ever used in this way, but there are plenty of other uses for it.

The foul owl – the disapproving orange owl you see when someone's account has been suspended.

Civilian – someone who's not a celebrity. As in, 'I'm following a range of celebrities and civilians.' A term that would no doubt enrage Twitter's original techie users.

Bot – a software application that runs an automated task over the Internet. In the case of Twitter, these are used to automatically generate messages from an account.

Mistweet – a tweet sent by mistake, or one you subsequently regret.

Backchannel account – a secondary account that's set up when someone wants to use Twitter for two distinct purposes. For example, someone might want to keep their straight-laced business persona and their messy personal life separate.

Ego-surfing – searching the web for mentions of your name or the name of your company. To do this on Twitter, you can sign up to a service like TweetBeep or go to http://search.twitter.com/advanced, which lets you filter tweets by content, user, place and date.

Qwitter – someone who gives up on Twitter as soon as it's served the purpose they wanted it to. Some would accuse Barack Obama of this, though I suspect he's got more important things to do now.

Abbreviations you might see

Given that tweets are restricted to 140 characters, it's no surprise that acronyms and abbreviations abound on Twitter. Here are a few you might see, but bear in mind that some tweeters believe that if you use too many you're effectively cheating.

RT – Retweet. An update that's being republished so it can reach more people. This might be because it promotes an event or links to a site or just because it's an interesting tweet. If you feel like retweeting, be careful to make sure you don't have all the same followers as the original tweeter, as they'll see the same message twice.

OH – Overheard. To quote something you overheard in real life, type 'OH' and the thing you overheard in quote marks. Usually used anonymously, to quote an unusual snippet of conversation you've eavesdropped.

HT – Heard Through. When you've found out about something through someone else in real life, and you want to acknowledge them. Like retweeting a conversation.

DM – Direct Message. A private message you can send to anyone who's following you.

IRL – In Real Life. Used to refer to that strange place where you have to look at actual people rather than screens and communicate by opening your mouth and making noises with it, or something like that.

OMG – Oh My God. Another ubiquitous online acronym, this one can make you sound like a hyperactive teenager and belongs in tweets like 'OMG!! Josh just looked at me!! He is sooo cute!!'

NSFW – Not Safe For Work. Often used to warn you that a link contains porn or offensive material, so don't click on it if you're in the office. Unless your screen faces the wall, of course.

LOL – Laughing Out Loud. One of the most widespread acronyms in online and text speak, this is as common on Twitter as any other social networking site, but considered annoying by some. Especially if you use a variation like 'mega LOLZ!!!'

ROFL – Rolling On Floor Laughing. For when even mega LOLZ is inadequate to describe how much you're laughing at the clip of a panda sneezing. Other variations include BL (Belly Laughing), BWL (Bursting With Laughter), FOMCL (Falling Off My Chair Laughing), LMAO (Laughing My Ass Off), LSHMBH (Laughing So Hard My Belly Hurts), LTM (Laughing To Myself), SWL (Screaming With Laughter) and the nuclear option, ROFLMAOWPIMP (Rolling On Floor Laughing My Ass Off While Pissing In My Pants). This last option should only be used if you can't imagine anything funnier than the thing you're currently commenting on. Remember – if something even funnier happens, you will have nowhere else to go.

How to decide if you want to follow someone back

'I will follow you if you follow me,' as Phil Collins so memorably sang. But is Phil's advice good when it comes to Twitter? Should we follow someone back just because they're following us?

Not necessarily. Look at their profile and decide if you'd want to see their tweets in your timeline. They might have found you through a common friend, or a topic that you've tweeted about. On the other hand, they could just be playing a numbers game, trying to follow as many people as possible in the hope that they'll get followed back and build a profile that makes Tom from MySpace look like a hermit.

Take a look at the kind of links they're posting. Will these be useful to you, or will they spam you with the same link in every update?

Look at their ratio of following to followers. If they follow thousands people but few people follow them back, it's not a great sign. Glance through their profile to see if they send many @ replies. If they do, it's a good sign that they're using Twitter to engage with others. Unless all their replies are things like, 'Dude, that is so gay', in which case they're a troll, and you should block them. And check how many updates they've posted in total. If they've only ever managed a handful, they're unlikely to make much impression on your timeline.

And finally, do they have an attractive model as their profile picture and a link to cheap Viagra in every single tweet? Then it's probably better not to follow them. I know this should go without saying, but someone must be falling for it.

Tweet yourself clever

If you're a true twitterholic, you're probably incapable of reading anything over 140 characters long. As a result, you'll miss the greatest works of literature ever produced. But don't worry, I've reduced some of them into tweets so you can savour their emotional richness too.

Hamlet
williamshakespeare Danish guy's mum marries his murdered father's brother. He sees his dad's ghost. Everyone dies. Fail.

about 400 years ago from first folio

Paradise Lost
johnmilton Satan is cast down from heaven. God tells Adam and Eve not to eat apple. They eat apple, get it on and are thrown out of Eden. Epic fail.

about 340 years ago from ten books

The Canterbury Tales

geoffreychaucer Pilgrims tell each other stories while walking from London to Canterbury. Includes fart jokes. LOL!

about 600 years ago from fragments

The Bible

god I created the universe, sent my carpenter son to earth, you killed him, but he's coming back soon. I've got 2 billion followers ;)

about two millennia ago from manuscript

The God Delusion

richarddawkins @god you don't exist and everyone should unfollow you.

about three years ago in reply to god

The Catcher in the Rye

jdsalinger Rich kid thinks everyone
is fake except for his little sister.
Has breakdown. @markchapman
is now following @johnlennon

about 60 years ago from hardback

The Great Gatsby

fscottfitzgerald Jay Gatsby <3 Daisy
Buchanan. Makes $$$ throws parties
and looks at green light. They get together.
Gatsby and American dream die.

about 80 years ago from hardback

The Da Vinci Code

danbrown Professor of symbology tries
to solve a murder by following clues
around touristy locations in Europe.
Very few paragraphs are longer than tweets.

about six years ago from airport bookshop

Great Expectations

charlesdickens Orphan given £££ by secret follower. He thinks it's @misshavisham but it turns out to be @magwitch

about 150 years ago from periodical

Pride and Prejudice

janeaustin Woman meets man called Darcy who seems horrible. He turns out to be nice really. They get together.

about 200 years ago in three-volume hardback

Bridget Jones's Diary

helenfielding RT @janeaustin Woman meets man called Darcy who seems horrible. He turns out to be nice really. They get together.

about 10 years ago in paperback

Clarissa, or the history of a young lady: comprehending the most important concerns of private life and particularly showing the distresses that may attend the misconduct both of parents and children, in relation to marriage

samuelrichardson 18th-century writer takes 1536 pages to tell us about a young woman falling for a cad. You can't even fit the title into a tweet.

about 260 years ago in seven sodding volumes

Wuthering Heights

emilybronte Catherine Earnshaw marries Edgar Linton but really loves Heathcliff *sigh*

about 160 years ago from false username EllisBell

Lady Chatterley's Lover

dhlawrence Upper-class woman gets it on with gamekeeper. NSFW.

about 80 years ago from underground edition

Waiting for Godot

samuelbeckett Vladimir and Estragon
stand next to tree and wait for Godot.
Their status is not updated.

about 60 years ago from French version

Ulysses

jamesjoyce Man walks around Dublin.
We follow every minute detail of his day.
He's probably overtweeting.

about 90 years ago from journals

Finnegan's Wake

jamesjoyce Riverrun, past Eve and Adam's,
from swerve of shore to bend of bay . . .
WTF???!!!????

about 70 years ago, from journals

Moby Dick

hermanmelville Ishmael and Ahab
get disrupted by fail whale.

about 160 years ago from three volumes

77

You know you're a twitterholic when . . .

Here are thirty warning signs that you might be getting addicted to tweeting. If they sound familiar, it might be time to go offline and read a book or whatever it was we used to do before the Internet existed.

1. You've tweeted more than ten times in one hour.

2. You've tweeted more than fifty times in one hour.

3. And you were pottering around the house at the time rather than attending a tech conference.

4. You can't bring yourself to look at MySpace and Facebook because you feel guilty that you've been ignoring them.

5. You check Twitter before your email when you turn your computer on.

6. You use Twitter search more than Google.

7. You've tweeted while driving.

8. You've written a note of something you want to tweet later because you couldn't access your phone or computer at the time.

9. You've learned to perform complex tasks with one hand so you can tweet with the other.

10. You've noticed that everything you ever write, from greetings cards to tax returns, is restricted to 140 characters.

11. You get upset and wonder what you're doing wrong if your follower number goes down.

12. A celebrity tweeter is following you back.

13. And the moment you found out was the highlight of your year.

14. You restrict your tweets to 120 characters, to give them a better chance of being retweeted.

15. You tweet more words than you speak out loud every day.

16. Tweeting is always the first thing you do in the morning and the last thing you do at night.

17. You've burnt a meal or let a bath overflow due to tweeting.

18. You've tweeted about having a serious accident before getting round to calling the emergency services.

19. You compulsively hit the refresh button every time you're looking at a website.

20. You get annoyed at the poor netiquette of Twitter newbies.

21. You spend more time looking at your girlfriend or boyfriend's profile than at them.

22. You're on the tweetwasters.com hall of fame.

23. You've checked Twitter on the way back from the bathroom in the middle of the night.

24. You've got out of bed at night because you've thought of something to tweet, and you know you won't be able to sleep until you've posted it.

25. You've introduced yourself to people in real life with your username.

26. You've got more than one Twitter account.

27. You've sent an @ message from one account to another.

28. You've sent a direct message from one account to another.

29. You always tweet while watching TV.

30. And this doesn't even feel like multitasking anymore.

'Twitter is the messaging system that you didn't know you needed till you had it.'

Biz Stone, co-founder of Twitter

Tweeting from your phone

Sick of being told to switch off your computer and stop wasting your life on Twitter? Then tweet from your mobile, so you can waste your life on Twitter wherever you are.

As part of the registration process, Twitter gives you the option to link a mobile phone to your account, allowing you to tweet and get replies, messages and updates by SMS. But, as a bit of small print might say, your standard text messaging rates will apply, and notifications aren't available on every network in every country. Alternatively, you could sign up to Twe2 (twe2.com), which sends you an SMS whenever you get a direct message or a reply. It's free, but the text messages have ads at the bottom of them. Which will really add insult to injury if you get a spam tweet.

If you're tweeting by SMS, you can use the following designated commands to perform particular functions:

ON – turn on all phone notifications on.

OFF – turn all phone notifications off.

STOP or QUIT – stop all messages to your phone.

ON username – turn phone notifications on for this user.

OFF username – turn phone notifications off for this user.

GET username – find someone's most recent update.

@username – send a public message or reply to someone.

D username – send a direct message to someone.

WHOIS username – find profile information for someone.

FAV username – mark someone's last tweet as a favourite.

STATS – find your number of followers and following.

INVITE – type this command and then someone's phone number and they'll get an SMS invitation to Twitter.

Mobile tweeting really comes to life, though, when you're using a phone with 3G or wi-fi. Mobile sites like m.slandr.net, m.dabr.co.uk and Twitter's own m.twitter.com work well, but downloading an application for your handset is worth the effort. Some of the most popular include Twitterrific for iPhone, TwitterBerry for BlackBerry, Twitdroid for Android G1 and Twibble for various Nokia phones. All of these apps have slightly different features, but generally speaking they make it easier to do things like reply, retweet and post photos. Twitterrific, for example, lets you flip through tweets using the iPhone's touchscreen, but you'll have to fork out for a premium version if you don't want to see ads in your feed.

Once you've installed your chosen mobile application, you'll begin to see the true possibilities of Twitter: blogging your life in real time, broadcasting to thousands of followers from the bus stop and sharing interesting things you see as Twitpics. But with this new power will come potential hazards. For a start, you will now be in even greater danger of twitterholism. You might start to notice angry faces appearing just above your phone in your field of vision. These are the people who are trying to speak to you in real life.

A further hazard is that you'll be more susceptible to drunken tweeting. A tweet like 'Hey ladiez!!! There's a party going down!!! Oh yeah, itz on!!! Who wantz it???' might seem witty and sophisticated in the bar, but could cause embarrassment the next day. Remember, if you're too drunk to play Tetris or Solitaire on your phone, you're too drunk to tweet on it.

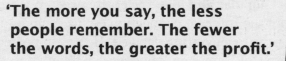

'The more you say, the less people remember. The fewer the words, the greater the profit.'

Francois Fénelon,
eighteenth-century French theologian

Celebrity tweets

Recently, celebrities have been piling onto Twitter as though it was a green room full of cocaine. And unlike in the real world, you won't get a restraining order filed against you if you follow them. Here are some of the most notorious twitterati.

Ashton Kutcher
Username: aplusk

You'd think that if the *Dude, Where's My Car?* star wanted to step out the shadow of famous wife Demi Moore, he might do some decent acting or something. Instead, he's decided to become the most popular and inane celebrity tweeter, whining about the Internet connection on his yacht and his private jet getting delayed. He's even posted a Twitpic of Demi bending over in a bikini alongside the tweet 'Shhh don't tell wifey'. Some thought that Kutcher was cleverly devaluing the paparazzi by invading his own privacy. Others thought that Kutcher just found it funny to post a picture of an ass.

In a well-publicized contest with CNN Breaking News, Kutcher's account became the first to get over a million followers, forcing Twitter's original techie users to wonder, 'Dude, where's my social networking service?'

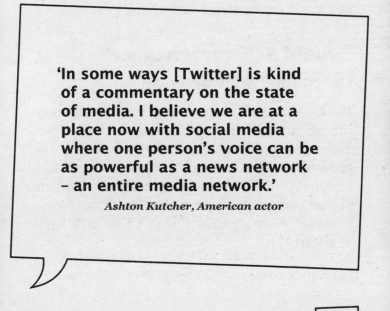

'In some ways [Twitter] is kind of a commentary on the state of media. I believe we are at a place now with social media where one person's voice can be as powerful as a news network – an entire media network.'

Ashton Kutcher, American actor

John Mayer
Username: johncmayer

The singer-songwriter famously used Twitter to express his heartbreak about splitting up with Jennifer Aniston. His tweet 'This heart didn't come with instructions' made some wince, but if it saved the world from a tortuous heartbreak ballad, then we have even more reason to thank Twitter.

Arnold Schwarzenegger
Username: Schwarzenegger

The Governor of California regularly tweets about education bills and environmental initiatives, but drops disappointingly few *Terminator* references. I know he wants to be taken seriously as a politician now, but would it kill him to put 'My mission is to protect you' as his bio, or tweet 'I'm altering my timeline'? Even signing off with 'I'll be back' would be a start.

P Diddy

Username: iamdiddy

The bloated egos of hip-hoppers and the boasting potential of Twitter were always going to be a messy combination, but Puffy's real-time narcissism still needs to be seen to be believed. At one point, he even claimed to be tweeting during a ten-hour tantric sex session, although we all know that his actual bedroom tweets would probably read like this:

iamdiddy Rolling over and going to sleep!!!

about a minute ago

iamdiddy Getting it on!!!

about two minutes ago

iamdiddy Taking a honey back to my hotel room!!!

about three minutes ago

89

While all of this was probably just a hoax to goad gossip bloggers, it could still be part of a horrifying celebrity trend. The last thing we want is Chris Moyles or Rosie O'Donnell sending us sexually explicit tweets and making us vomit all over our keyboards.

Snoop Dogg
Username: snoopdogg

The gangsta rapper refers to his account as his 'twizzle', which sounds more like something Jamie Oliver would tell us not to eat than a social networking platform. Sadly, despite the playa lifestyle Snoop details in his raps, his updizzles tend to be rather mundizzle.

Britney Spears
Username: britneyspears

Spears has been prime tabloid fodder for years, but her Twitter account has failed to deliver the real-time breakdown that ghoulish fans were hoping for. So far her followers have been treated to an obviously ghost-written overview of her activities. Things seemed to be getting more scandalous at one point, when Spears tweeted that her vagina was '4 feet wide with razor sharp teeth'. But this was just the result of hackers getting into her account.

I'm not quite sure why anyone would want to do this, though. I mean, how dare anyone out there make fun of Britney after all she's been through!!! All you people care about is readers and making money off of her!!! She's a human!!! LEAVE BRITNEY ALONE!!! Sorry, I thought I was that guy from YouTube for a minute there.

Stephen Fry
Username: stephenfry

Given how long most of the words he uses are, it's surprising that Fry has become such a fan of micro-blogging. But following Fry has become pretty much a Twitter mandatory, especially in the UK. After all, where else this century will you be able to see expressions like 'crumbs', 'bally' and 'tish, fie and pish'?

Jonathan Ross
Username: Wossy

A true twittervangelist, Jonathan Ross has probably done more than any other British celeb to wrestle Twitter out of the clammy hands of the tech community and thrust it into the mainstream. Ross interacts frequently with his followers, setting challenges such as suggesting an unexpected word for him to drop while hosting the Baftas ('salad' was chosen). It's also entertaining to watch his enemies at the *Daily Mail* spin his innocuous tweets into proof that he's a menace to society and should be removed from it. Like when Ross tweeted 'I am very polite in person. I'm just not very good with answering machines', and the *Daily Mail* managed to drag this 14-word tweet into a 500-word article with the headline 'Shameless Jonathan Ross Still Joking About Andrew Sachs Messages'.

Russell Brand

Username: rustyrockets

Ross's 'Sachsgate' accomplice is also widely followed, though tabloid editors will be disappointed with the lack of scandal in his updates. If he tweets about being in bed with Morrissey, he's probably referring to his cat rather than the singer, but we can hope.

MC Hammer

Username: MCHammer

Hammer has a surprisingly large number of followers who are presumably interested in harnessing the power of social media to buy parachute pants. But it could be worth joining the ranks of Hammerfans, if only because getting a tweet from him might be the only time you get to genuinely use the words, 'Stop. Hammertime.'

Evan Williams, Biz Stone and Jack Dorsey

Usernames: 'ev', 'biz' and 'jack'

The co-founders of Twitter have an unsurprisingly massive amount of followers. In fact, Williams is so popular that, according to *Rolling Stone* magazine, he once tweeted that he was craving chocolate and then found that some had been left on his doorstep. Williams's tweets are often surprisingly frank, as when he called a woman in front of him in a queue a 'bitch' because she had described Twitter as boring. It's not clear what exactly upset him here – the fact that the woman was complaining about his company or the fact that he's got half a million followers but people still don't recognize him in the supermarket.

Neil Gaiman

Username: neilhimself

The Sandman and *Coraline* author seems to spend most of his time in airports or at book signings, which must come as a disappointment to his legions of goth fans who would prefer to imagine him applying eyeliner, hanging around graveyards dressed in black and floating through dreams.

Lance Armstrong
Username: lancearmstrong

The seven-time Tour de France winner is such a dedicated tweeter that it wouldn't surprise me if he posted the update 'I'm just coming up to the finishing line now. Crossed it! I won!' However, getting constant updates of his intense training schedule might make you feel a bit guilty as you sit in front of your computer dribbling cheese from a stuffed-crust pizza down your shirt.

Armstrong even used Twitter to try and recover his bike after it was stolen from him in February 2009, which certainly shows his faith in social networking. Although Craigslist and eBay are surely the most useful sites to go to if you've had something like that nicked.

David Lynch

Username: DAVID_LYNCH

Similarly, fans of the Twin Peaks director might feel let down that he doesn't post things like 'hanging out with dancing, backwards-speaking dwarf in Black Lodge.' What he does post, though, are very detailed weather reports broken up by musings like 'the art of living is the real art'. Which, in its way, is even weirder.

Shaquille O'Neal

Username: THE_REAL_SHAQ

Anyone who tells you that Twitter is only for nerds should be forced to read the profile of basketball player and 'Shaq Fu' inventor Shaquille O'Neal. Shaq has hundreds of thousands of followers, and most of them have never even been near a spell check, let alone a *Star Trek* convention.

Barack Obama
Username: BarackObama

It's no surprise that Obama, who has been described as the 'first Internet president' has a Twitter account, and that he's one of the most followed people on there. Obama posted over 200 updates as part of his election campaign, climaxing with 'We just made history', which is probably the most important tweet ever. Except for that one about what Ashton Kutcher had for breakfast.

Since then he's been pretty quiet, leading some to brand him a 'qwitter' for dumping Twitter as soon as it served its purpose. But if anyone can legitimately use the excuse that they're too busy to use it, it's him. Plus, what exactly do these people want him to tweet? 'About to launch secret attack on Taliban! Check out the Google Map http://tinyurl.com/etc'? 'Just met Kim Jong-il. What a douche, LOL'? 'Just changed nuclear launch codes to 1843174057'?

Twitter celebrity scandals

Wherever celebrities go, scandal follows, and so it has proved with Twitter. But rather than drink driving and hookers, most Twitter scandals have revolved around whether the celebrities in question are genuine or not.

Twitterjacking

In the early days of Twitter, most of these scandals were about tweeters impersonating celebrities through fake accounts. Known as 'twitterjacking', this practice is popular with lonely people who like to run a practical joke into the ground months after it's stopped being funny. It's reasonably harmless in the case of the many people claiming to be George W. Bush (make this even semi-literate and you've given the game away) but can be upsetting for the celebrities being imitated. Stars such as Ewan McGregor, David Tennant, Maya Angelou, Eddie Izzard and Keith Chegwin have all had to issue statements distancing themselves from bogus accounts, and the website valebrity.com was set up to identify genuine celebrities on Twitter. While some fake accounts are clearly intended as parodies, others are so detailed you might reach the disturbing conclusion that the people who maintain them actually think they are the celebrities in question.

Ghost-tweeting

In order to combat twitterjacking, many celebrities now have an official Twitter presence, which they link to from their websites. But even if you're looking at these official accounts, you can't be sure if they're actually responsible for the words you're reading. The issue of ghost-tweeters recently came to public attention when the *New York Times* revealed that rapper 50 Cent was having tweets written for him. Suspicions were raised when Fiddy tweeted, 'My

ambition leads me through a tunnel that never ends.'
Given that the most sophisticated metaphor Cent
had managed previously was 'I love you like a fat kid
love cake' in the track '21 Questions', some wondered
whether this was all his own work. It transpired that
the words had actually been typed by Chris Romero,
who runs the rapper's website, although he claimed
that he was paraphrasing an interview and that 'the
energy of it is all him'. While it's understandable that
celebrities might turn to ghost-writers for help with
full-length autobiographies, it's pretty sad if they
can't even manage a sentence all on their own. What
next? Paying someone to speak and move for you so
you can sit still all day in a massive bathtub full of
money?

Another danger of ghost-tweeting is that the
person employed to do it for you might be an
idiot. Actor Hugh Jackman was recently forced to
apologize after apparently referring to Sydney Opera
House as the 'Opera Center' in a tweet. Outraged
by his ignorance, the Australian press confronted
Jackman, who was forced to admit that his tweets
are actually written by an American publicist. He's

just lucky they didn't tweet, 'Looking at the Great Barrier Reef, throwing a shrimp on the barbie and playing my didgeridoo, you flaming galah.'

One-way tweet

Even the accounts that are written by the celebs themselves have come under attack. The gossip site HolyMoly.com recently accused celebrities of using Twitter as an easy way to 'get their ego stroked so they can bask in the glow of their popularity' rather than to interact. They even devised a spreadsheet of the top 'self-obsessed twits' by comparing numbers of followers to following. The spreadsheet certainly looked convincing, and few could argue that Russell Brand, Katy Perry, Lily Allen, Ashton Kutcher and Chris Moyles didn't deserve their top five placings. But the method of statistical analysis is highly suspect here. Just because a celebrity isn't following many people, it doesn't mean they're not using Twitter to interact with fans. They could still be responding to @ messages from their followers. In fact, if you're a fan of a tweeting celebrity, you've got a much better chance of a response if you send them a question via Twitter than if you email them through their website. Or wait outside their gated mansions with a flask full of coffee and a look of undying love in your eyes.

Of course, many would question if it really matters whether celebrities are using Twitter to broadcast rather than interact. Expecting celebrities to automatically follow you back is like pulling up a chair next to them in a restaurant and getting offended when they don't want to be your friend.

For Twitter's hardcore techie users, the celebrity invasion has marked a huge dumbing-down and a betrayal of the principles of social networking. But for most, it's been another aspect of Twitter than we're free to enjoy or ignore. If we want to use Twitter for real-time micro-blogging at Apple conferences, we can. And if we want to use it to find out that Britney Spears has just bought a handbag and a new pair of sunglasses, we can do that too.

The strangest twittersonas

If you're sick of trying to work out if a celebrity's updates are genuine or written by their PR people, why not follow some tweets that can't possibly be genuine? Thousands of accounts have been set up for fictional characters, pets and inanimate objects. Here are a few of the oddest:

Don Draper from *Mad Men*
Username: don_draper

The online world was outraged when cable channel AMC asked Twitter to suspend a number of accounts that fans were writing as characters from the series *Mad Men*. Ironically for a show that's about advertising, the network had failed to understand that this micro fan fiction was promoting the show for free. Realizing their mistake, the network allowed the accounts of characters such as Don Draper to be re-activated and fans were once again free to be transported back to a time of chain-smoking, hard-drinking sexism. Or as it's known in Alabama, the present day.

Darth Vader
Username: darthvader

It's a sad truth that the Dark Lord of the Sith has more followers on Twitter than Yoda, Obi-Wan Kenobi and Luke Skywalker put together. I suspect that Vader's simply using some kind of mind trick here that his rivals are too good to adopt. If you find that your cursor is drawn towards the 'Follow' button against your will when you look at Vader's profile, report him immediately.

The Joker
Username: the_JOKER

Batman's archnemesis has been tweeting from inside Arkham Asylum for a few months now. It's fairly typical of the asylum's lax security that a psychopathic supervillain such as the Joker should be afforded Internet privileges. While I'm sure he'll claim that his interest in social media is genuine, I have no doubt that he's secretly hatching a plan to leak green gas out of keyboards and send us all into debilitating fits of laughter while he escapes and takes over the world.

God
Username: god

It can't be easy to answer the question 'What are you doing?' when you're everywhere at once, but at least God tries. Nice to know that the deity still finds time to let his flock know what we should be doing from time to time. Even if it transpires that what we should be doing is looking at clips of people falling over on YouTube.

Jesus
Username: kingofthejews

The King of the Jews has an account, but he's given a disappointingly small amount of updates since he set it up. He's probably just embarrassed because his dad's on Twitter too.

Satan
Username: satan

Want your soul cast down into a fiery lake of burning sulphur where the smoke of your torment will rise up for ever and ever? Then check out Satan's profile and click on the 'Follow' button. At first it seemed as though the Prince of Darkness was embracing Twitter as an efficient new soul-harvesting platform, but his updates have tailed off a little recently. He's probably gone back to putting subliminal messages in heavy metal songs.

Andy Stanford-Clark's house
Username: andy_house

IBM inventor Andy Stanford-Clark has hooked up
his house so it tweets updates on its energy use.
If you've ever wanted to become close, personal
friends with a building, this is the account to follow.

The Ghost of Peter
Username: ghostofpeter

As the website pettweets.org verifies, an alarming
number of people are posting on behalf of their
pets. If this wasn't creepy enough, ghostofpeter is an
account set up for a cat that died in 2002. Twitter
tip: if you click on someone's profile and everyone
else they're following is a dead animal, it might
be wise to block them. Or at least hold back from
sharing your home address.

The Natural History Whale
Username: NatHistoryWhale

Perhaps the most popular dead animal on Twitter is the whale on the ceiling of the Natural History Museum in New York. The mammal's tweets mix whale facts with observations about the crowd milling about below and angry references to Japanese and Icelandic whalers. It's nice to see a positive representation of the species on Twitter after all the anger that the fail whale has caused.

A Tomato Plant
Username: startrkplant

Already following some buildings and dead animals? Maybe it's time to follow a tomato plant. This account is actually less eccentric than it sounds, as it's merely a plant hooked up to a 'Botanicalls Kit', which sends you a tweet whenever it needs watering. As such, it only tweets 'Water me please' and 'Thank you for watering me'. It still makes for more interesting reading than Britney Spears's account, though.

Ten other accounts worth following

As well as following celebrities, imaginary people and objects, you can also follow hundreds of services and news channels on Twitter. Here are ten worth a look.

CNN Breaking News
Username: cnnbrk

Pretty essential if you're so addicted to tweeting that you don't even look at the news anymore, and the only way you find out about major stories is from the reactions of other people on Twitter. The last thing you want is for global apocalypse to break out, and you only find out about it because your friend tweets, 'Nuclear missiles falling from sky. Grrr!'

109

Secret Tweet
Username: secrettweet

A service that lets you anonymously share your deepest and darkest secrets with thousands of strangers on Twitter. Go to secrettweet.com, post your confession in the text box, and it will be sent to the account's followers. The secrets range from the tragic, like a man who admits the Internet is his only friend, to the disturbing, like the mother who claims to have walked in on her son masturbating to *Star Wars*. Let's just hope for his sake that it was Princess Leia's slave girl costume and not Chewbacca's all-over body hair that inspired the five-knuckle shuffle.

Twitter tips
Username: Twitter_Tips

A service that sends you links to articles about Twitter and new applications. Useful if you want to transform yourself into a social networking guru and become one of the huge number of people who use Twitter just to talk about Twitter.

Bad Movie Club
Username: badmovieclub

Followers of this account are given a bad movie to watch at a particular time so they can tweet their disappointment with it. Since badmovieclub organized a showing of M. Night Shyamalan's unintentionally hilarious *The Happening*, followers have been organizing their own events using the hashtag #badmovieclub. Why not arrange a bad movie club event of your own next time a Nicholas Cage film is shown on TV?

TwitterLit
Username: TwitterLit

This account tweets the first sentences of books and then posts an Amazon link. Perfect for those who enjoy reading, but find that their attention tends to tail off after about six or seven words.

Mr Tweet
Username: MrTweet

Like a less socially awkward version of Friend Finder on Facebook, Mr Tweet suggests people for you to follow based on who you're currently following, the links you post, and the content of your tweets. Rather camply billing itself as 'your personal Twitter assistant', Mr Tweet sends you reports with its suggestions, as well as an overview of your 'twitteristics', such as how often you tweet, how often you send @ messages and how often you post links.

Qwitter
Username: iquit

A service that uses Twitter to shame you into giving up smoking. Message @iquit every time you have a cigarette, and it will add up your total per day on a progress graph. An interesting idea that could be tailored to treat many other addictions. Except for twitterholism, obviously.

The Onion
Username: TheOnion

It's no surprise that the world's funniest website is also the world's funniest Twitter account, and it's heartening to see that *The Onion*'s spoof news updates are more followed than most serious news sources. Admittedly, following their account will get you nothing more than their latest headlines with links to the articles in question, but at least you'll be the first to read them, and first to expose those who attempt to pass off *The Onion*'s jokes as their own.

TrackThis
Username: trackthis

A service that allows you to track UPS, Fedex and DHL packages over Twitter. Send it your tracking code and it will send you a direct message whenever your package changes location. Just don't start messaging your packages back. That would be weird.

Remember the Milk

Username: rtm

A service that turns Twitter into a to-do list when used in conjunction with an account set up at rememberthemilk.com. You can direct message it with things you want to add to your to-do list, or reminders you want to receive at certain times. Perfect for people so addicted to Twitter that they forget to eat, sleep or leave the house.

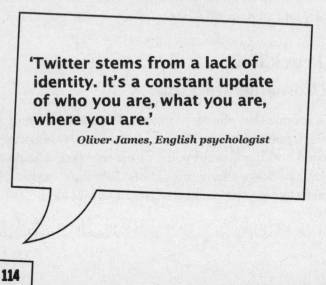

'Twitter stems from a lack of identity. It's a constant update of who you are, what you are, where you are.'

Oliver James, English psychologist

The ten commandments of Twitter

The Internet God hath asked me to pass on these commandments to you. Obey them or thou shalt be cast down to Twitter hell, where every screen shall display the fail whale forever.

1. Thou shalt interact.

2. Thou shalt not spam.

3. Thou shalt tweet when thou hast something worth tweeting about.

4. Thou shalt not continue thy messages over multiple tweets. What dost thou think this is, thy blog?

5. Thou shalt honour thy Stephen Fry.

6. Thou shalt not steal. Thou shalt retweet instead.

7. Thou shalt not LOL, unless something's really funny. Like, thou art snorting coffee out of thy nose or something.

8. Thou shalt not turn every @ message into a link to thy blog.

9. Thou shalt not follow false idols. Only those idols who write their own tweets rather than getting their publicists to do it for them are worthy of thy attention.

10. Remember the followfriday and keep it holy.

'Twitter says: I want to be in contact with you, but not too much. It's the equivalent of sending a postcard.'

Alain De Botton,
philosopher and television presenter

Marketing on Twitter

The good news is that Twitter can be useful for promoting anything from your blog to your company's product. The bad news is that using it properly requires effort.

Lots of companies seem to think that all they have to do is set up a Twitter account, tile a photo of their product as a background design, follow as many people as possible and then sit back and watch the sales graph climb. But do this and you could get blocked as a spammer, even if you're promoting something more useful than cut-price Viagra.

The principles of using Twitter for marketing are much the same as for personal use. If you interact with people by replying to their tweets, you'll have a much greater presence than if you just use Twitter to broadcast. If you tweet about general events in your field rather than just posting about yourself, people will be much more likely to follow you. But if you turn every tweet into an excuse to link to your site, it's unlikely that many people will be interested. If you must link to your page, make sure you at least flag up what it is in your tweet. You don't want to come across like one of those spammers who misleads us into thinking we're about to see something interesting while really linking to an incomprehensible oriental website about fake Gucci handbags.

Use Twitter's search function to find out what people are saying about you or your competitors. Their opinions might not be nice, but they could be useful to know. You should consider posting a reply if you think someone is making an unfair comment. Unless that person is obviously a massive douchebag who moans about everything, in which case ignore them.

Try to use Twitter to build up a community of people who are interested in your area. Follow relevant people, comment on their tweets, retweet what they're saying, and you'll get the right kind of followers. There's no point in setting up a profile and then getting the work experience boy to click 'Follow' on as many accounts as he can before he gets a blister on his finger. You might end up with a few thousand followers, but most of these will be accounts that automatically follow back and they won't really be listening. In fact, many of them will also be trying to use Twitter for marketing, and you'll all be uselessly barking pitches at each other in your own online ghetto while under the impression that you're embracing social media.

Ultimately, Twitter can be a rewarding promotional tool if you take the time to use it properly. But if all you want to do is jump on the bandwagon and blast random people with your aggressive self-promotion, you might as well write your tweets down on a piece of paper and stuff them in the shredder.

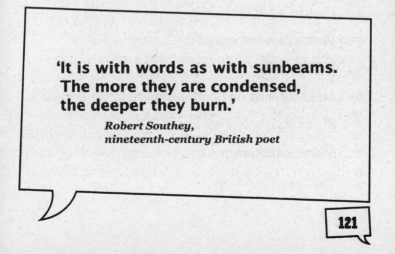

'It is with words as with sunbeams. The more they are condensed, the deeper they burn.'

Robert Southey,
nineteenth-century British poet

Tweeter's block

What are you doing? If your honest answer to this question would be, 'Sitting in front of Twitter and trying to think of what to write', you should remember that tweets don't always have to be status updates. If you've having trouble deciding what to tweet, here are twenty suggestions to get you going.

1. Link to a website.

2. Link to a new blog post.

3. Link to a photo.

4. Link to a news story.

5. Link to a YouTube clip.

6. Link to a song on Spotify, Blip.fm or Grooveshark.

7. Share an interesting fact.

8. Share a quotation.

9. State your opinion.

10. Disagree with someone else's opinion.

11. Report a problem with a product or service.

12. Make a prediction.

13. Congratulate someone.

14. Post an open invitation to an event.

15. Ask your followers a question.

16. Answer a question someone else has asked.

17. Set a contest for your followers.

18. Review a film, album, book, product or service.

19. Recommend some good accounts to follow.

20. And if you still can't think of anything to tweet, go on then, tell us what you're eating.

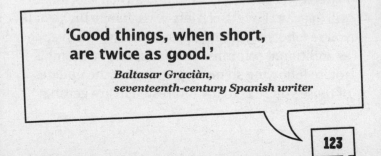

'Good things, when short, are twice as good.'

Baltasar Graciàn,
seventeenth-century Spanish writer

Twitter tools

Ashton Kutcher and P Diddy aren't the only tools you need to know about when you start tweeting. Although you can enjoy most of what Twitter has to offer from the comfort of your homepage, there are a number of tools, sites and apps that can enhance your experience.

TweetDeck
http://www.tweetdeck.com/

A Twitter desktop client that organizes your activity into columns such as timeline, replies and direct messages. Click on the speech bubble icon and a textbox you can tweet from and a URL shortener will appear. TweetDeck lets you arrange the people you're following into groups, which will then appear as additional columns. This is especially useful if you're following so many people that the updates of those you're actually interested in are getting lost. TweetDeck features buttons for retweeting, replying, direct messaging, translating, searching, following and unfollowing. It will play an automatic notification sound whenever one of your followers tweets, which is an incredibly dangerous feature for Twitterholics, who should click on 'Settings' and disable it if they're to have any chance whatsoever of logging off and going to bed. It also has a function that lets you share video clips of 12 seconds from your webcam or mobile, which is useful if you talk as fast as someone from a 1940s screwball comedy, rather than Cleveland from *Family Guy*. Other Twitter desktop clients worth a checking out include Twitterlicious, Twitterrific, Snitter, Twhirl, Nambu and Tweetr.

Twitpic
http://twitpic.com/

A site that lets you share photos on Twitter through your phone or computer. Just enter your username and password and click on the 'Upload photo' button. You'll also find that Twitpic is included in many desktop and mobile Twitter clients. Some people view Twitpic as a vital new tool for 'citizen journalism', which allows tweeters to distribute real-time photos of important events from their phones. Others, such as Aston Kutcher, have used it as a vital new tool for showing everyone their wife's arse.

Twistori
http://twistori.com/

A site that publishes tweets anonymously in an auto-updating feed based on the keywords 'love', 'hate', 'think', 'believe', 'feel' and 'wish'. The site claims to be a social experiment, although if it is I'm not sure what conclusion to draw except that most people love being drunk and hate being at work. Nonetheless, this is an oddly addictive site that is a bit like plugging your brain into the Cerebro computer from *The X-Men*. Except that instead of detecting super-powered mutants, it detects teenagers who love *Twilight* and hate school.

126

Tweetburner

http://tweetburner.com/

An example of a URL shortening site, which help you cram long links into short tweets. Just copy and paste the URL into the textbox on the site to shorten it. Tweetburner can also track how many people are clicking on the links you're creating, which is useful if you're using Twitter for marketing or if you just want to know exactly how many people clicked on that link of the fat kid falling over on the dance mat that you posted.

My Tweet 16

http://www.mytweet16.com/

Enter anyone's username and this site will show you their first sixteen tweets. They might be social networking superstars now, but the chances are that when they started they were hopeless n00bs like everyone else, and their first tweet was, 'I'm just trying out this new Twitter thing', followed ten minutes later by, 'Why has no one contacted me yet? I don't understand what all the fuss is about.'

TwittyTunes

http://www.foxytunes.com/twittytunes/

TwittyTunes makes it easier for you to tweet about the music you're listening to. It features a text box with 'Listening to' followed by the name of the track you're listening to on a media player such as iTunes, and a button that lets you post this information as a tweet. This might be worth doing if you want to show off your obscure taste in afrobeat, post-rock or free jazz. But there's not much point if you're just going to tweet about how you're listening to Coldplay and Radiohead like everyone else.

Twittervision

http://twittervision.com/

A site that shows you where things are being tweeted from on a world map. The 3D version, which shows the location of tweets on spinning globe, is the closest you'll get to feeling like a psychic alien floating around the world without taking any illegal substances.

Qwitter

http://useqwitter.com/

As well as being the name of a service that can help you give up smoking through Twitter, Qwitter is also the name of a service that emails you when someone stops following you. Enter your username and email, and when you get unfollowed, you'll be sent a message in this format . . .

username stopped following you on Twitter after you posted this tweet: 'Just found button under bed. Not sure what shirt it goes with, but don't really want to throw it away. Any ideas? http://twitpic.com/etc'

'Using Twitter suggests a level of insecurity whereby, unless people recognize you, you cease to exist.'

Dr David Lewis,
British cognitive neuropsychologist

TwitterSnooze

http://twittersnooze.com/

If one of your friends is flooding your timeline with unwanted updates, but you think they might be upset if you unfollow them, TwitterSnooze lets you temporarily unsubscribe to their account. Of course, there's no guarantee that your overtweeting friend won't still be offended, but if they're attending an insurance conference and they're only tweeting to keep themselves awake, I'm sure they'll understand.

TweetWasters

http://tweetwasters.com/

A site that tells you exactly how much time you've spent on Twitter. As with this kind of option on computer games, you don't really want to know. Features an alarming hall of fame of people who either don't sleep or have learned to tweet while doing so.

TweetLater

http://www.tweetlater.com/

A site that lets you schedule tweets to be sent at certain times, which will obviously be more useful for people using Twitter as a promotional tool rather than as a real time mini-blog. It also lets you send out an automatic message of thanks to new followers (but be warned that some regard this as bad netiquette, especially if your heartfelt message of thanks features a link to your blog, website, podcast or new 100 per cent safe life-changing miracle weight-loss pill).

Twitterfox

http://www.twitterfox.net/

A Firefox extension that pops up in the bottom right of your browser and displays new tweets, replies and messages. Install this and your chances of getting through that lengthy online article you wanted to read for work are pretty much zero.

Twitzer
http://shorttext.com/twitzer.aspx

A Firefox extension that creates a link to further text if you exceed the 140 character limit, so that your update will read something like, 'In Subway eating 6-inch toasted meatball marinara with double cheese, onions, sweetcorn, peppers, lettuce, tomato... http://shorttext.com/etc' Needless to say, Twitter purists will regard this as a serious breach of netiquette that entirely misses the point of micro-blogging.

Twollo
http://www.twollo.com/

An automatic 'find and follow' service. Enter your Twitter account details and a list of topics you're interested in, and the service will follow people who've been tweeting about them. Useful if you're using Twitter to find hundreds of people with similar hobbies or professional interests, but use it sparingly or your stream will descend into randomness and you might as well look at the public timeline instead.

That's What She Said

http://thatswh.at

You know a catchphrase has become uncool when there's a site dedicated to tweets containing it. This site collects all the double entendres that have inspired the reply, 'That's what she said', the standard joke of Michael Scott from *The Office*. So now you can follow unintentional smut like, 'It's so huge', 'That was so hard', and 'I didn't expect to be doing this all night' as it's uttered. Looks like we'll have to go back to using 'as the actress said to the bishop' or 'f'nar f'nar'.

Tweetbeep

http://tweetbeep.com/

A service that sends you updates whenever someone mentions your name, your blog, your company or your website. Useful for businesses that want to keep track of their customers or just for paranoid people who are convinced that everyone's tweeting about them behind their back.

Tweetsmarter
http://tweetsmarter.com/

A site that allows you to insert symbols such as hearts, smileys and stars into your tweets. If these kind of things excite you, perhaps you should avoid polluting Twitter with them and stick to MySpace, where you'll be able to find colourful, glittery, animated variations that will excite you even more.

Twtpoll
http://twtpoll.com/

A site that lets you conduct a poll among your followers by submitting a question and a series of options. You can use it to ask the social media elite about the future of Web 2.0, or you could use it to ask the guys from the comic convention who they think would win in a battle between Wolverine, Robocop and a Dalek.

Ping.fm
http://ping.fm/

A site that lets you update all your social networking services simultaneously. Post and update on Ping.fm and it will appear on Twitter, MySpace, Facebook, Bebo, LinkedIn, Friendfeed, Friendster, Tumblr or whichever one is fashionable this week. While this can save you the hassle of typing the same update more than once, it doesn't really allow for the fact that people use different social networking services for different aspects of their life. Plus, Twitter terminology like @, RT and #followfriday will spill over onto Facebook and confuse your grandparents when they check their accounts.

> **'Therefore, since brevity is the soul of wit, and tediousness the limbs and outward flourishes, I will be brief.'**
>
> *William Shakespeare*

Ten types of Twitter twat

Here are ten types of people who should be banned from ever going near a computer or phone again for crimes against tweeting.

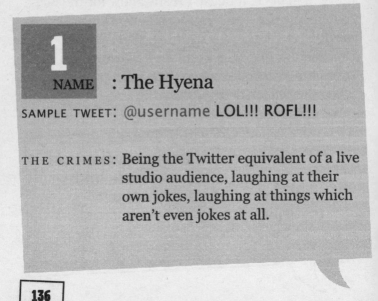

1

NAME : The Hyena

SAMPLE TWEET: @username LOL!!! ROFL!!!

THE CRIMES: Being the Twitter equivalent of a live studio audience, laughing at their own jokes, laughing at things which aren't even jokes at all.

2

NAME : The Slowcoach

SAMPLE TWEET: @username Check out this cool site for finding things on the Internet: http://www.google.com

THE CRIMES: Catching on to sites light years after everyone else has grown sick of them, posting 'hilarious' links which turn out to be that fat kid singing along to Numa Numa, only recently discovering *The Onion*, and spending the next few years Rickrolling.

3

NAME : The Spammer

SAMPLE TWEET: @username Great photos!!!
Check out these photos!!!
http://www.cheapviagra.com

THE CRIMES: Sending out off-topic @ replies just
to send out their URL, following
thousands of people but posting few
updates, pretending that they just
won a free iPod, telling us how we
can get 16,000 followers in 90 days
and generally being evil robots.

4

NAME : The Lifestreamer

SAMPLE TWEET: Coffee is slightly too hot to drink. I'll wait a couple of seconds for it to cool down.

THE CRIMES: Listing every mundane detail of their life, confirming the prejudices of Twitter-haters and generally suffering from diarrhoea of the keyboard.

5

NAME : The Professional Parent

SAMPLE TWEET: Daniel is eating his favourite – spaghetti and meatballs . . . http://twitpic.com/etc

THE CRIMES: Listing every mundane detail of their child's life, boasting about their ability to breed as if they were the only people in the world who had it and, quite probably, owning a 'Baby on Board' sticker for their car.

6

NAME : The Traveller

SAMPLE TWEET: Can't believe I'm getting a signal on Machu Picchu! Just updated South America section of my travel blog http://tinyurl.com/etc

THE CRIMES: Assuming that their endless updates from exotic, distant places will make us feel jealous as we read them from our moribund open plan offices, and being right.

7

NAME : The Stalker

SAMPLE TWEET: @username That's a nice blue dress you're wearing today.

THE CRIMES: Remembering you from school and believing that you're still close friends, turning up at social functions mentioned on Twitter that they weren't invited to, sending @ replies to all your tweets, and thus forcing you to find out how to block users and turn account settings to private.

8

NAME : The Show-off

SAMPLE TWEET: Relaxing in the pool with Naomi Campbell and Kate Moss at @iamdiddy's party.

THE CRIMES: Boastfulness, ego-stroking, making everyone eagerly await a reversal in their fortunes so we can laugh in their smug faces.

143

9

NAME : The Numbers-game Player

SAMPLE TWEET: Help me get 15,000 followers by midnight!!! Please RT!!!

THE CRIMES: Treating Twitter like a video game where your number of followers is your score.

10

NAME : The Troll

SAMPLE TWEET: @britneyspears You suck Britney!!! BITCH!

THE CRIMES: Leading such a lonely existence that the only way they can get anyone to interact with them at all is to start an argument, generally being total dickwads.

Further uses for Twitter

There's more to Twitter than telling your followers what's on your mind or spamming everyone about your blog. Here are a few unusual ways in which people have used it.

Switch the light off

In May 2008, Justin Wickett posted a clip on Vimeo explaining how to Twitter-enable your home. In it, he shows how he's connected the Insteon light switches in his house to his laptop, so he can send tweets from his phone and turn the lights on and off. Thanks to him, the hideously outmoded practice of tweeting, 'I'm going to switch the lights off', and then getting up to do so is a thing of the past. We can at long last do both at once.

Lose your job

A Californian woman who was recently offered a job by Cisco Systems tweeted that she was weighing the benefit of 'a fatty paycheck against the daily commute to San Jose and hating the work'. A Cisco staff member who saw the tweet replied, 'Who is the hiring manager? I'm sure they would love to know that you hate the work.' The job offer was withdrawn and 'Cisco Fatty' became a legendary mistweet and a cautionary tale for all those who blurt out such thoughts without setting their account to private. If you have a technophobe manager who still needs the IT guy to help them underline things in Word, you might get away with moaning about them on Twitter. But if you work for an IT multinational, it's probably best to keep your bitching to yourself.

Propose

In October 2008, Sean Bonner tweeted, 'So, um, wanna get hitched?' to his girlfriend, Tara Brown. After what must have been a tense eighteen minutes for their followers, Tara replied, 'Yes.' A couple of weeks later, they tied the knot and posted their wedding video to YouTube. Disappointingly, though, they made eye contact and spoke their vows out loud rather than tweeting them on their iPhones.

Recharge your laptop

Although there's no button on Twitter that will magically transmit electricity to your computer, you could post a tweet to see if anyone can lend you a power cable. That's what Guy Kawasaki did in September 2008 when his MacBook needed an emergency recharge. Within moments several of his followers had offered to come to the rescue. Admittedly, this is easier when you've got over 100,000 followers like Kawasaki. Most of us can't even get the guy who sits next to us at work to lend us one.

Write your autobiography

The website booktwo.org has demonstrated how to publish all your tweets as a hardback book. Judging from the example they've done on the site, you'll end up with something that looks more like an experimental novel than an autobiography. Which is fine as an unusual exercise in vanity publishing, but let's just hope that mainstream publishers don't get any ideas from this. The last thing we want to see is Tesco stocking up on piles of Russell Brand's *My Tweety Weets* or Jonathan Ross's *The Best of the Mr Pickles Tweets, Volume Four*.

Hoax the Twitter community

Hoaxes on Twitter are sometimes even more sophisticated than teenagers in Pittsburgh pretending to be Katie Holmes so they can tweet, 'I am being held against my will! Please send help!' Some hoax tweets have been plausible enough to go viral on Twitter. Like 'Pay Per Tweet', a service announced on the 1st of April 2008 (like, duh) by ProBlogger, which claimed it would give you money to retweet messages from advertisers. Or the 'Premium Account' hoax on BBspot, which claimed that for just $250 a month you could update your character limit to 500 and get three celebrity followers of your choice. It's surprising how many people fell for this and posted angry replies, though most of them claimed they were merely trying to perpetuate the hoax when the penny dropped.

A further high-profile April Fools' prank was played in 2009 when the *Guardian* announced that it would be the first newspaper in the world to become a Twitter-only publication. The prank seemed to be making some kind of point about shallow online content distracting people from in-depth journalism. At least, I think that's what it was saying. I only bothered to read the first couple of sentences before I went back on Twitter.

Travel the world

In March 2009, Paul Smith attempted to travel from England to New Zealand relying entirely on the goodwill of Twitter users. Without a single penny to spend on transport and accommodation, Smith was given lifts, ferry tickets, plane tickets, bus tickets and beds to sleep in all the way across Europe and the US. Cannily, Smith has found a way to conduct a worthwhile social media experiment while at the same time getting away with being a massive freeloader.

Write a novel

Anyone who doubts the potential of Twitter to inspire creativity should check out the novel *Washington Stone: Action Gynaecologist* created by Daniel O'Brien using the hashtag #Twitbook. This way they can have their prejudices confirmed and feel smug. O'Brien invited eighty of his friends to co-write the book on Twitter, one tweet at a time. The result was an unreadable and puerile story about a man with a penis made of ham who gets attacked by a swarm of pitchfork-wielding Bruce Campbells. It was still more believable than most Dan Brown novels, though.

Write a short short story

Who needs to post a story over multiple tweets anyway? One hundred and forty characters is more than enough to establish a compelling protagonist, a credible series of obstacles to overcome, a satisfying middle act full of unexpected twists and turns, a fulfilling conclusion and a heart-warming epilogue. Use the hashtag #flashfiction or #vss to find stories written in single tweets, or to attempt one yourself.

Write poetry

Given the 140-character limit, it's not surprising that the haiku is the most popular poetic form on Twitter. Type in the hashtag #haiku and you'll find people who give their updates about going to the shops or cooking dinner a strange profundity by arranging them into lines of five, seven and five syllables. If you find this form too restrictive, you could post a longer poem one line at a time, like the Nigerian writer Ben Okri has done. Or if that sounds like too much work, you could simply print off your last ten tweets, take them down to your nearest 'poetry slam' and read them out in a suitably serious voice. Your brave, experimental work will move everyone in the room to tears.

Cook a meal

The *Sunday Telegraph* recently challenged celebrity chefs such as Raymond Blanc and Rowley Leigh to write recipes as tweets to see if Twitter could be used as a cookery book. Most of them did a pretty good job, although it's unlikely that fine cuisine will replace takeaway pizza as the true twitterholic's food of choice. Maybe if they bring out an iPhone with a microwave function . . .

Hack into a high-profile account

Like online banking, Twitter has been plagued by 'phishing', the practice of sending an email directing someone to a false login site so they can find out their password. Unlike online banking, however, hackers won't make any money out of doing this on Twitter. But they can send out a rude message to someone's followers, and then point at their screens and snigger. This hacking epidemic explains why Fox News tweeted, 'Bill O'Reilly is gay', CNN anchor Rick Sanchez tweeted, 'I am high on crack', and Barack Obama apparently wanted his followers to take part in a survey and 'win $500 in free gas'. Cue lots of overweight single men typing ROFLMAO on message boards.

Pretend you've got millions of friends

Some cynics would say that this is all any social networking service is ever used for. But if you really want to know what it would be like to be friends with everyone in the world, go to twitter.com/public_ timeline and keep pressing refresh until your browser deliberately crashes just to make it stop. It won't be long before you realize that being friends with everyone in the world would be like being mad. Is this really what you want your timeline to turn into, you people who treat Twitter as a numbers game?

Become a fan of a porn star

The capacity of the adult entertainment industry to embrace new technology should be an inspiration to all sectors of business. You wouldn't think that 140 characters of text was a medium with much erotic potential, but hundreds of porn stars are now on Twitter, posting updates of their sexual shenanigans with all the enthusiasm of grocery store clerks working sixteen-hour shifts. You can choose to follow them if you don't mind everyone being able to see this on your profile. Which you probably should.

Get out of jail

When journalism student James Karl Buck was arrested in Egypt for taking photos of an anti-government demo, he tweeted about it from his phone. Within hours his followers had notified the American Embassy and Buck was freed. So next time someone says that Twitter's only good for finding out what Lance Armstrong had for breakfast, tell them it could mean the difference between freedom and ending up as someone's prison bitch.

The ten social net-working sites they should create next

After Twitter and the micro-blogging trend, where will the next online craze come from? Here are a few suggestions. If they make you a web billionaire, just buy me lunch or something.

Sylabl

As online content continues to expand, we won't have time to type or read 140 characters any more. This is where nano-blogging site Sylabl comes in. With updates restricted to a single syllable, you'll be able to read updates such as 'Glad', 'Sad' and 'Meh' from every single person in the world.

Body Trackr

In fact, why bother with things as old fashioned as words at all? Body Trackr uses a sensor in your iPhone to broadcast your current posture to followers around the globe. And no need to bother with emoticons any more, Body Trackr will automatically update your followers by SMS when your facial expression changes.

Witter

On the other hand, isn't it about time that long-winded people had a network too? Witter allows you to post updates of 14,000 characters or more. You can describe exactly what you're doing in tedious detail and share this information with others who have difficulty cutting to the chase.

Stalkbook

Many people criticize social networking sites for encouraging stalkers, but what if you're a Z-list celebrity who actually wants to attract some? Just create an account, link it to the GPS on your mobile and you'll have a flock of lonely oddballs following you in days.

Fakebook

A site that detects when someone you want to impress such as a girlfriend or potential employer is looking at your homepage and makes you seem more popular and successful than you really are. Contains features such as exaggerating the amount of friends you've got and generating pictures of you on luxury holidays.

Trollr

Under new Internet laws, anyone caught deliberately being a douche just to piss everyone off on a social networking site will be banished to Trollr. The site lets users share unfriendly, negative and contrary comments with each other, and displays an 'over capacity' error message every seventeen seconds.

Sim Celebrity Friendship

Some people will tell you that Twitter is just for sad and lonely individuals who like to pretend they're friends with celebrities. That's not true, but now you come to mention it, there could be a market for that. Post your updates onto Sim Celebrity Friendship and within seconds, celebrities as diverse as Madonna, Tom Cruise, Al Gore, P Diddy, Bill Gates and Tiger Woods will comment on them. And how is this possible? Because all the celebrities are computer simulations. Except for Al Gore. That's actually the real Al Gore. He's got a lot of time on his hands.

SpamFinder

Somebody somewhere must be responding to spam. This service collects all these gullible idiots and puts them in one place so scammers and aggressive marketers can contact them directly twenty-four hours a day, and leave the rest of us alone. To set up a SpamFinder account, just enter your username, password, postal address, email address, phone number, online banking password, mother's maiden name, sort code, PIN, credit card number and expiry date, details of where you keep your spare key and when you tend to be out of the house.

LinkedOut

Link your laptop, desktop and mobile to this site, and it will destroy them all, allowing you to have some peace.

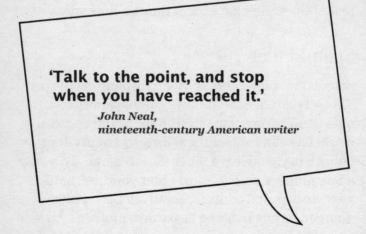

'Talk to the point, and stop when you have reached it.'

John Neal,
nineteenth-century American writer